1 MONTH OF
FREE
READING

at

www.ForgottenBooks.com

By purchasing this book you are eligible for one month membership to ForgottenBooks.com, giving you unlimited access to our entire collection of over 1,000,000 titles via our web site and mobile apps.

To claim your free month visit:

www.forgottenbooks.com/free75823

ISBN 978-0-484-40651-2
PIBN 10075823

A

SERMON,

DELIVERED AT

SHREWSBURY,

BY JOSEPH SUMNER,

JUNE 23, 1812,

THE DAY WHICH COMPLETED

𝔉𝔦𝔣𝔱𝔶 𝔜𝔢𝔞𝔯𝔰

FROM THE TIME OF HIS INDUCTION INTO THE

PASTORAL OFFICE,

OVER THE

Church and People in that Place.

....

SECOND EDITION.

PRINTED AT WORCESTER, BY WILLIAM MANNING.
JULY, 1819.

A

SERMON,

DELIVERED AT

SHREWSBURY,

BY JOSEPH SUMNER,

JUNE 23, 1812,

THE DAY WHICH COMPLETED

𝔉𝔦𝔣𝔱𝔶 𝔜𝔢𝔞𝔯𝔰

FROM THE TIME OF HIS INDUCTION INTO THE

PASTORAL OFFICE,

OVER THE

Church and People in that Place.

....

SECOND EDITION.

PRINTED AT WORCESTER, BY WILLIAM MANNING.
JULY, 1819.

SERMON.

PSALM cxlv. 4.

ONE GENERATION SHALL PRAISE THY WORKS TO ANOTHER, AND SHALL DECLARE THY MIGHTY ACTS.

THE works of God are a glorious and continued display of his perfections. Day unto day uttereth speech, and night unto night sheweth knowledge of God. The works of creation and providence loudly proclaim, through all the earth, his wisdom and his power. The work of redemption more abundantly manifests his grace and his mercy. This has employed the thoughts, the tongues and the pens of patriarchs and prophets—of apostles, and many other devout men, in various ages of the world. This has been the admiration and joy of saints and of angels, and will be celebrated in their united songs through all eternity. The works of creation, providence and redemption exhibit the glories of Deity to men, and teach them their duty to Him. Hence the importance of handing down, from one generation to another, these works of God, that they may excite our reverence and fear of Him—our gratitude and praise—our hope and trust. These important purposes are directly promoted by *sacred*, and are aided by all authentick history. Nations which are not favoured with divine revelation, possess much knowledge of the works and ways of

God, which Divine Providence enables them to transmit from one generation to another. In every age God endows some with super-eminent talents, to perform distinguished services in the world ; and he raises up others to be the historians of their deeds : and with these, they also register many of the dealings of God with the children of men, for the benefit of succeeding generations.

The works of God call for the notice and praise of his rational offspring, because they tend to the glory of the Creator, and to the instruction of his creatures. It is suitable at all times to praise God for his works, and to speak of him for the improvement of the rising generation; but there are certain periods in the revolutions of years, when it is proper to take a retrospection of the great events in providence, that we may impress our minds with the recollection of those providential dispensations, which have been conveyed to us by sacred and profane history, to strengthen our own faith and hope in God, and to establish these in others. It is also our duty to register and to declare those works of God, which have been exhibited to our view, while we have been upon the stage of action. In this manner, one generation should praise God's works to another, and declare his mighty acts.

This day completes half a century since my induction into the pastoral office over the church and people in this place. This connexion must soon be dissolved; and I therefore desire to direct your attention,

I. To some of the advantages, which result from the declaration of the works of God by one generation to another.

II. To notice the principal events that have taken place among us, during my ministry, particularly those which had an immediate relation to the inhabitants of this town. I shall close the discourse by a few reflections, as the application of our subject.—Permit me,

I. To direct your attention to some of the advantages which result from the declaration of the works of God, by one generation to another.

The communication of important knowledge from one generation to another, is one principal design of sacred history, which preserves the knowledge of the state of innocence, in which God originally placed man—of his fall from this state ; and of the provision made for his recovery. We cannot but admire the wisdom, power and goodness of the Creator in the formation of·man, in whose composition earth and heaven were united. A body formed of earth and wonderfully constructed, and a spirit of understanding given by the inspiration of the Almighty. We are justly astonished, when we contemplate the wonderful method devised and executed for the recovery of the race of mankind from the state of ruin into which, by their transgressions, they had plunged themselves. The historical part of scripture, and indeed the whole of the sacred writings, is one continued history of the work of redemption by Jesus Christ. The knowledge of the interposition of God in favour of fallen man was at first conveyed by tradition, one generation declaring the works of God to another, for which the longevity of those early generations was favourable. Unity of design, steadiness of co-operation, and a progress of discovery respecting the great designs of God towards man, were carried on from Adam to Noah, from Noah to Abraham, and from Abraham to Moses—one generation declaring the works of God to another. Moses compiled that part of the most ancient, the most elegant, and the most instructive of all books, which contains the history of the world from the creation to his own time. After him, numbers were raised up to continue the history of the dispensations of Providence with the Jews and some neighbouring nations, with which they had occasional intercourse, for the space of two thousand years. All these dispensations were intended to prepare the world for the appearance of the Messiah, concerning whom many predictions are interspersed in the sacred writings, and of whom sacred history gives many types, in the characters of men who were distinguished by a greater measure of gifts and graces, exhibiting to the world examples of human excellence, as patterns for our imitation. Hence we are called to notice the faith of Abraham, the innocence of Joseph, the meekness of Moses, and the patience of Job.

We also derive much information respecting the dispensations of Divine Providence from authentick profane history ; every page of which tends to confirm the sacred truth, that a wise, powerful and benevolent Being governs the universe—who brings good out of evil, and order out of confusion. History teaches us, that the powers and efforts of men and of nations are often directed to purposes very different from the original intention and design. The same Being made the greatest things and the smallest : all are parts of the same system ; and what appears to us the most inconsiderable, answers a useful end—as our Saviour observes, not a sparrow falls to the ground without the permission of God, and the very hairs of our heads are numbered. As nothing was made in vain, so nothing comes to pass without the appointment or the permission of God : some purpose therefore is intended by every thing that happens, as well as by every thing that is made. A design may not be so apparent in small things as in great; but the hand of God is really in every event which happens, and a recognition of past events is a source of useful instruction and improvement; for it will be the means of increasing our knowledge of God and of his works. What above all discovers the hand of Providence, as well as the weakness and short-sightedness of man is, that great events are often brought about contrary to the intention of the persons who were the principal instruments of them, and by the very means which were designed to produce contrary effects. Thus persecution has always been the means of promoting the persecuted religion, insomuch that it has become a common proverb—" The blood of the martyrs is the seed of the church." On the contrary, the success and prosperity of a nation have often proved the means of their ultimate ruin. In like manner, small events, and such as had no apparent connexion with the effect produced, have been over-ruled to bring about the greatest changes. Thus the desire of Henry VIII. to be divorced from a wife, was the means to produce the reformation in England, for which Protestants to this day rejoice.

Monuments erected in commemoration of great events are all fading, and mouldering into dust. Monumental inscriptions, which are intended to perpetuate the names of men who were greatly distinguished, as instruments in the important events of the world, are also perishing. It is the faithful page of history only that hands down to posterity the great events of the world, or the men who were conspicuous actors in them. Here the knowledge of them may be acquired, while the smallest vestiges of literature shall remain upon earth.—I pass,

2. To notice the principal events that have taken place among us, during my ministry, particularly those which had relation to the inhabitants of this town.

The last fifty years, perhaps, include as many important changes as the same space of time in any period of the world. North-America, half a century ago, was harmoniously connected with Great-Britain, and the latter was then closing a vigorous war with France and Spain. In the former part of that war we were unsuccessful; but in the latter part, Providence greatly smiled upon us—the British dominions were enlarged; and, by the conquest of Canada, this country was delivered from the terrour of an inimical neighbour. In consequence of this great event, our country promised itself long peace and rest. The most favourable opportunity was then offered to increase our settlements, extend our borders, and multiply our resources. Although these then provinces of the British empire had no design of becoming a separate nation, yet Divine Providence was preparing the way for this great event. An extensive territory on the north and west, which, at the close of the French war, was ceded to Great-Britain, with a chain of fortresses originally erected for our annoyance, at the acknowledgement of our independehce was included within the limits of the United States. This territory extends our national frontier, increases our conveniences, and adds to our security.

A perfect calm in the political world is not long to be expected. The reciprocal happiness of Great-Britain and the Colonies was too great to be of long duration. Soon after the peace of 1763, trouble came from an unexpected quarter. Great-Britain claimed a right to tax the Colonies without their consent, "in all cases whatever," and the claim gave general alarm. The opposition made to the encroachment upon American liberty was so far successful, as to keep back the dispute between the two countries from coming to the last extremity for about ten years; in which time we were rising in strength for an appeal to the Arbiter of the Universe, by the sword. A long and distressing war ensued, which cost the lives of many worthy citizens. Some of us still remember the gall and wormwood of those years, during which scarcely a family escaped the bitterness of having some friend slain in battle, or perishing in captivity. When we look back upon those scenes, in which we were either actors or spectators, we cannot but wonder, that the infant Colonies, so unprepared as they were for war, should dare to engage with one of the most powerful kingdoms of the earth; and at an early period of the contest to assume a name and a place among free and independent nations. But the Divine counsels must and will stand. That was the time appointed by Heaven for a nation to be born in a day; and circumstances were made to concur for its accomplishment. The situation of this country, from its first settlement by Europeans, has been very different from that of most others. In them, territory has been obtained by conquest, and government established by the sword. In this, the soil was purchased of the original inhabitants, and cultivated by the owners, who, when they could no longer be governed under the British crown, agreeably to their native privileges, framed a government for themselves, and established it by mutual consent; in all the concerns of which Heaven favoured them, and under which they, for a time, greatly prospered.

Half a century ago, the number of inhabitants in the district of country which now composes the United States, was small in comparison with our present numbers. The increase of husbandry, navigation and commerce, has been in full proportion to the population; and all these, since the revolution, have increased beyond example. At the close of the revolutionary war, the navigation of this country was next to nothing; but, within twelve years, the American flag was displayed in the ports of almost every commercial state and kingdom upon the globe; and, had not the spirit of enterprize been checked by commercial embarrassments, we cannot calculate the degree of wealth and respectability to which these United States would have arisen by this time. New settlements have been greatly extended, and four or five new states have been added to the original thirteen. Settlements have been made, churches formed, academies and colleges founded and put into a flourishing condition, where, less than fifty years ago, it was a howling wilderness. The wilderness has become a fruitful field, and the desert made to blossom like the rose. "Thus the period has been replete with events in our own country, which have astonished the careful and wise observers of Divine Providence in human affairs," which the historick page will declare to posterity; and in which future generations may trace the agency of the Almighty in the support of his church in the world.

From America the spirit of liberty was carried into France; but it could not there flourish. That nation was not prepared to entertain it. Upon throwing off monarchy, they fell into anarchy, and have been constrained at last to submit to a military despotism. Instead of ameliorating their condition, they have rendered it seven-fold worse than it was before. This might have been expected; for, under the influence of atheistick philosophy, they destroyed the constitutions of their religion, trampled upon the temples and the worship of their God; and they declared death to be an eternal sleep. An aspiring chieftain seized the favourable moment to usurp dominion; and he has established an absolute despotism over the nation. Not satisfied with the sceptre of France, he has spread desolation among the nations of continental Europe; and by intrigue and the sword has subjected many of them to a state of abject slavery. How far he may be permitted to go, and how long he may be permitted to be a scourge to the earth, God only knows.

But the compass of one discourse will not permit me to wander among the nations to declare the works of God. These all in a wonderful manner display his power, wisdom and goodness. In every country there have been distinguished characters raised up, who have proved great blessings or great curses to the nations which gave them birth. They who have been great and extensive blessings in their day ought to be remembered with respect. Many such, whose names are enrolled in the records of this country, were brought upon the stage of publick life during the last half century, and took their several parts in our revolution; most of whom have done their work, and have passed off. There have been many in the private walks of life, whose memory may be as precious to us as that of those who moved in a publick sphere, whose example may be as worthy of imitation, and the copy more extensively useful. The general on the field of battle, and the statesman in the cabinet, may exhibit something worthy the notice and imitation of those who may act in a like capacity; but to the generality of mankind it is a copy they do not aspire to write after. It is the industrious, prudent man, in private life, who sustains the character of an affectionate husband, a tender parent, a kind neighbour, a good member of society, and, which crowns all, of a good Christian, who sets an example for general imitation; and this copy may be useful for mankind at large. In many respects the state of society, within the last fifty years, has been improved. Civilization has been extended, and knowledge increased. The slave-trade has been discountenanced within the United States, and in the northern states slavery is wholly laid aside; and we are told that the condition of slaves in the southern states, as well as in some other parts of the world, is made better. They are not only provided with more comfortable food, but a degree of attention is paid to their religious instruction, and some of them are christianized. These circumstances give us reason to hope that the time is approaching, when all God's rational offspring will enjoy civil and moral freedom.

During the period within our review, invention has been upon the stretch in this country. Many useful discoveries have been made in the mechanical arts, by which much labour is saved, and greater dispatch made. Another occurrence, which strongly characterizes this period, and exhibits a still more favourable appearance respecting mankind, and the church of God is, the charitable exertions that are making to spread the gospel in our infant plantations, and among

the heathen. For these apostolick and glorious purposes numerous societies have been formed ; and they
give great encouragement to all who have any interest
at the throne of grace, to pray for the bringing in of
the Jews, with the fulness of the Gentiles, that when
the people of God take pleasure in the stones, and favour the dust of Zion, that *He* would arise and build
her up.

But as smaller events become important to those,
who, by their local situation, have an immediate interest in them, I would notice some things respecting the
church and flock of God in this place, and more particularly those which have taken place within the last
fifty years. Some of these may be worthy of attention, as they may excite your gratitude to Heaven
for the smiles of Divine Providence upon the inhabitants of this town from generation to generation. We
have it from good authority, that the land which originally composed the town of Shrewsbury, was passed
over by the proprietors of the adjacent towns, because
they thought it not worthy of being taken into their
grants. Hence the form of it was irregular. But a
governing Providence had not destined this tract to
remain a waste. In process of time it was to become
a fruitful field. In 1717, it was granted to a body of
men, who were not only enterprizing and industrious,
but also religiously disposed. They considered publick worship and the publick institutions of religion to be
of the first importance, in their tendency to promote the
highest interests of society, and to prepare men indi-
vidually for the kingdom of heaven. About the year
1721, the first meeting-house in this place was built
by the proprietors. On the fourth of December, 1723,
the church was gathered under the inspection of an

Ecclesiastical Council, which was convened for the purpose of ordaining the first minister of the town, the Rev. JOB CUSHING, who was called and settled by the proprietors; and who was distinguished for his prudence and general exemplary deportment. He died, suddenly, August 6, 1760.

The land in the grant which composed Shrewsbury, was originally rough, and it had been greatly impoverished by frequent burnings by the proprietors of neighbouring settlements. Much hard labour was necessary to bring it into a state of cultivation, and the progress of its settlement was consequently slow; but, from personal acquaintance with some of the first·settlers, and from correct information respecting others, I am authorized to say, that they were remarkable for their industry, frugality and temperance. It seems that they attended unto and embraced the doctrine inculcated in the first sermon that was preached in the plantation. It was delivered by the Rev. Mr. BRECK, of Marlborough, on the 15th of June, 1720, from the following words, viz.—"Righteousness exalteth a nation, but sin is a reproach to any people." It appears that they adopted the resolution of Joshua, that, as for themselves and their households, they would serve the Lord. The church when formed consisted of sixteen male members; and about an equal number of female members was soon after admitted into the church, most of them the partners of those who were first embodied. It appears from the church records, that within four years from the time the church was gathered, the heads of families, almost without exception, became members of it. The church remained in perfect harmony and peace for eight years, when some dispute arose respecting discipline, and particularly on the question, whether Ruling Elders be a distinct office appointed by apostolick authority ? This controversy continued about ten years, when a small number withdrew from the church; but they afterward returned, and remained regular members until the time of their death. This was the only controversy, as far as I can learn, which has ever arisen in this church. After the death of their first pastor, and before the ordination of the second, the church renewed their Christian obligations; and at that time they added one article to their covenant. This, after some years' experience, was found to be the ground of uneasiness to some members, and an objection, in the minds of numbers, against seeking admission into the church. The article was in consequence rescinded by an unanimous vote. During the fifty years of my ministry, the church has scarcely in any instance met, but for the management of its prudential concerns; and I have scarcely known a vote passed which was not unanimous.

In December, 1742, the north part of Shrewsbury was incorporated into a parish; and in the next year, fourteen male members of this church and sixteen female were dismissed and recommended by this church: these, with some others, were formed into a church state, on the 6th of October, 1743, when the first minister was ordained over the church and people of that parish. In March, 1786, this parish was incorporated into a town, by the name of Boylston; and in September, 1796, a second church was formed in that town, by a number of members from the first church, together with some members from the churches in Holden and Sterling; and this new society has since been incorporated into a town, by the name of West-

Boylston. Three houses for publick worship are now standing on the original grant of Shrewsbury.

This church, when it renewed its covenant in the year 1761, consisted of twenty-eight male members; the number of female cannot be ascertained: but the communicants were more numerous than the members of the church. Many who moved into town did not remove their relations from the churches which they originally joined, and become acting members of this body. This church, from the first, has manifested a candid spirit towards other denominations of Christians. They have never refused communion to Christian professors, whose lives and conversation, in the judgment of charity, supported their profession. Although emigration of church members, as well as of other inhabitants of the town, has been very considerable, yet the church has been gradually increasing in numbers. There have been ten officiating deacons in this church, since its formation. The two who were in office, when the second church was formed, fell within the limits of that society. There is but one individual now living in town, who was a member of this church at the time of my ordination; this is a female: and there are, I believe, but three persons now alive who were then members. Two hundred and sixty-seven have been admitted to full communion during my ministry, and about one thousand one hundred and twenty have been baptized. The births within this period were between thirteen and fourteen hundred. The number of marriages I cannot precisely ascertain. I have solemnized the marriage of four hundred and ten couple, the greater part of whom emigrated. The deaths have been about six hundred and fifty—between twelve and thirteen in a year. For some of the first years of my ministry, I cannot be answerable for the correctness of my bill of mortality. The average number of deaths in the year, since that time, has been a little more than one to an hundred of the inhabitants. According to the census in 1790, the population of the town then was nine hundred and sixty-three souls; in 1800, one thousand and forty-three; and in 1810, one thousand two hundred and ten. Thus hath God increased our numbers. Did the inhabitants of the town attend publick worship as universally at the present day as they did fifty years ago, this house would scarcely contain our assembly.

From the first settlement of the place, our people have been laudably disposed to make suitable provision for the education of the rising generation. Not a few have felt themselves able and willing to give some of their children more than a common school education; by which they have been qualified to become instructers in schools, and to serve their generation in various other useful departments. Twenty of our youth have received a collegiate education within the last fifty years, and three at an earlier period, many of whom became respectable ministers of the gospel; and others of them have been distinguished in important offices of the government.*

* The Hon. ARTEMAS WARD, Esq. was born in Shrewsbury, November, 1727, and graduated at Harvard College, 1748. Soon after, he received the commission of a Justice of the Peace. He was a field-officer in the French war, in 1758, and in 1762 was appointed a Judge of the Court of Common Pleas for this county, and in 1775, was constituted Chief Justice of this court; and for a time he filled the offiee of Judge of Probate for the county. For many years he was the Representative of this town in the General Court: he was chosen the Speaker of that honourable body, and he for several years filled a seat at the Council Board. When hostilities between Great-Britain and America were expected, the Provincial Congress of Massachusetts appointed him to command the forces of the Province; and at the commencement of the war, in 1775, he commanded the American army, near Boston, from April to July, when he was superseded in this arduous duty by General Washington. Under Congress he was appointed the

Few towns have been favoured with more general health than this for the last half century. The greatest number of deaths which has happened in any one year, took place in 1770. The canker-rash or throat-distemper then prevailed, and twenty-seven persons died by it. Two families lost four in each. In 1775, the dysentery was brought into this place from the camp, and proved fatal to numbers ; others of our inhabitants died of various disorders, and the whole number of deaths in that year was nineteen. These two were the years of our greatest mortality. A large proportion of our people have attained to a good old age, and some to a degree of longevity which, in modern times, is rarely the lot of humanity. JOHN KEYES, Esq. died March 3, 1768, at the age of ninety-four : he left a widow, who lived to be ninety-six years old, and they lived together in the married state seventy-two years. In 1790, one in fifty of our inhabitants had passed eighty years of age. Of these, one died in her hundred and fifth year,* and another lived to be an hundred and five years and two months old.† They who live the longest, find an appointed time beyond which they cannot pass. One generation passeth away, and another cometh. Every year makes changes in families, in churches, and in towns.

It is computed, that in this country, which is considered one of the most healthy in the world, one half of the human race die under twenty years of age. It is supposed, that in twenty-seven years as many die

second in command in the continental army, which commission he resigned soon after the British troops evacuated Boston. Under the old Confederation, he was chosen a Member of Congress, and was repeatedly elected a Member of the House of Representatives in Congress, after the establishment of the Federal Constitution. He continued in publick life until bodily infirmity obliged him to retire. He died October 27, 1800.

*Widow MARY JONES.   † Widow RUTH GARFIELD.

as are living at any given period of time. The whole population of the earth has been estimated, by some, at one thousand million. From these principles we may calculate, that about thirty-seven million persons die annually on our globe—seven hundred and twelve thousand every week—one hundred and one thousand seven hundred and fifty daily—four thousand two hundred and thirty-nine every hour—and about seventy every minute. This number of human beings is coming into and passing out of the world without intermission. "What an astonishing current of souls is rapidly borne on the tide of time, incessantly shooting into the ocean of eternity, and appearing before God in judgment!"* According to this calculation, the earth changes its inhabitants twice in a little more than half a century. When we compare our bill of mortality with the above estimation of the mortality of the world, it will appear very small; and we shall perceive our obligations to bless and to praise God for his goodness manifested towards us.

In this climate, healthy as it is, half a century makes great changes in the inhabitants of our land. It has changed all the ministers of the gospel in this extensive county; and very few remain in the Commonwealth who were in the ministry at the time of my induction into office. Thirty years have swept away almost all the leading characters in the revolution. Rulers and ruled, ministers and those to whom they ministered, are gone upon the current of time. If we look into families, we find very few instances where both the heads continue for fifty years. There are but two such families now in this town, which were here when I was ordained; and there are very few instances where either of those, who were then heads of families, remain unto this day.

*Rev. Dr. Trumbull,

APPLICATION.

The cursory review we have taken of the events of the last half century, naturally leads us to serious re_ flections. This period of time has been important— not because I, an unworthy minister of Jesus Christ, have been continued among you; but because it has been filled up with important publick events, and with concerns of great personal interest to you, indi- vidually, or in your connexion with domestick life. Almost every one of you can recollect, that within this period, a parent, a partner or a child has died. Not one of those years perhaps passed without events highly important to some of us. Few of us, who have not been called within these years, at different times, to take the place of mourners, and to follow divers of our friends to the silent mansion. Lovers and friends have been taken from us, and put far into darkness. We lamented their deaths. The worm- wood and the gall, our souls have still in remembrance. It is highly important that we inquire what effect those things have had upon us; whether they have awaken- ed in us a carefulness to prepare for our own great and last change.

When we look forward fifty years, they appear very long; but when we look back fifty, they appear very short. I cannot realize that so many years have rolled away since the day, when, with fear and trembling, I took the oversight of this flock, then solemnly commit- ted to my charge. It had been my intention not to en- ter into the ministry at so early a period; but it ap- peared to others, as well as to myself, to be the will of Providence that I should. I could not doubt the sin- cere affection of those who invited and solicited me to take the charge and oversight of them in the Lord. I have reason gratefully to recognize their candour and kindness to me during my more youthful years, and even as long as they were continued with us. But they are numbered with the congregation of the dead. Like candour and kindness I have reason to acknowledge in the present generation. I am sensible, that in such a long course of ministrations, the manner and method of a preacher usually become obsolete; and, I trust, that while any traces of reason remain with me, I shall not forget the kind reception I have met with from the body of this people. The unhappy habit, which some of this society have formed, of neglecting the publick institutions of religion, has been the greatest discour-agement which I have experienced since my settle-ment. This has caused me to entertain serious thoughts of discontinuing my pastoral relation to this church and people, in the hope that a new preacher would engage the attention of those who habitually absent themselves from publick worship, and bring them off from their dangerous neglect. But this, when I have mentioned the thought, has been universally condemned by those in whose wisdom and friendship I have been accus-tomed to confide. But my course is almost finished: according to the order of nature, my work is almost done. I have been with your predecessors, and with most of you, in seasons of trial and affliction. I have endeavoured to minister unto you according to my fee-ble ability, in private as well as in publick, agreeably to the revealed will of God. This I have taken for my guide, without enlisting myself under any dividing hu-man name. It has been my endeavour to preach Christ and Him crucified, and to inculcate the important du-ties of the Christian character. With what success and profit I have ministered, will more fully appear on another day; and, where no advantage has been derived from the means of grace in this place, it will then also appear who was the blameable cause. All I have to say is, that, as far as I know myself, I have endeavoured to fulfil the ministry which I have received of the Lord Jesus; and Providence has favoured me with such general health, that I have rarely failed in standing in my lot in publick, or of obeying more private calls to ministerial duty. If life, health and any tolerable degree of mental strength should be continued unto me a little longer, I shall be willing to spend these in your service. But I find the infirmities of age increasing upon me, especially mental infirmities: these may perhaps increase so fast, that I may not be sensible of my own decays: in that case, you will kindly prevent my attempting to minister unto you.

According to the course of nature, you must ere long be destitute of a minister; you will not therefore think it assuming, if I give you a word of advice respecting the re-settlement of a Christian pastor. You will not, I presume, be willing to live without the publick ministrations of the gospel. As you have a fund for the support of a Congregational minister, which cannot be alienated to any secular purpose, nor converted to the support of a minister of any other denomination of Christians, there can, I trust, be no doubt that on my decease, the pastoral office in this church will soon be re-filled. Still I feel anxiety lest divisions should arise among you. There are at this day dividing names, among which many preachers enlist: I therefore take the liberty to recommend the following things unto you. Let your waiting eyes be unto God, not only in secret and in private, but also in publick, with

humiliation and fasting. Take advice, especially of
the neighbouring ministers, who, it may well be supposed, have more acquaintance with candidates than you
can possess—then hear and judge for yourselves. Be-
ware of such preachers as place the essence of religion in external modes and forms, in dividing names,
or in speculative matters, in themselves doubtful, and
which would be useless if their truth could be made
certain. They, who enrol themselves as the disci-
ples of this or that distinguished man in the Christian
world, feel that they are pledged to support his peculiar
system ; and they call into exercise all their metaphysic-
al powers, to persuade the less informed that they see
further into hidden things than their fellow-men.

There is, I conceive, more danger of deception from
these metaphysicians than from those who make the
essence of religion to consist in external rites, or in a
mode of administering them ; because the latter at
first view, appear so absurd, and savour so much of a
pharisaical spirit, that none but the most uninformed
can be deluded by them. The Congregational society in this town, in their fund, possess the best barrier
against sectarianism and fanaticism. Professions are
cheap things, and many are willing to offer that which
costs them nothing. I urge upon you diligently to
search the scriptures, and to try every man's doctrine
by this standard. Place not your dependence upon the
creeds and confessions of men, nor upon any human
composition. If any man preach any other gospel
than that which you find in the scriptures, believe him
not. If the scriptures be not a sufficient rule of faith
and practice, we cannot expect to find this rule among
human forms. It will be a misapplication of the a-
vails of your funds, to apply them for such speculative

preaching, as tends neither to enlighten the mind nor
to regulate the practice. But, as none but professed
Congregationalists will have a right to a voice in the
choice of a minister here, I trust you will harmonize
upon this important subject. Having witnessed in
many places the unhappy consequences which result
from pushing the settlement of a minister, in opposition to a respectable minority, I cannot but caution
you against this errour. The spirit of party is hereby
excited, and an alienation of brethren ensues, which
requires a long time to remedy. In case of great divis-
ion, permit the individual who is the object of it, qui-
etly to depart, and invite a new candidate, looking to
God to unite you in his own time and way. Be not
too hasty in forming an opinion of your candidate, but
take time to satisfy yourselves respecting his *doctrine*,
his *morals*, and his *prudence*. Some appear better upon a slight acquaintance than they do when fully
known. It is the complaint of some societies, that
their ministers preach a different doctrine after their
ordination from that which they preached while candidates. You will therefore consider the importance
of as full an investigation as in your power of the in-
tegrity, the knowledge, in a word, of the various qual-
ifications for a minister, possessed by your candidate,
before you proceed to settle him.

The review of the last half century naturally leads us
to inquire, what probably will be our situation before
the next fifty years shall complete their revolutions.
What intervening changes may take place with us, or
any of ours, we cannot tell : what sufferings are allot-
ted us—what conflicts we may be called to sustain,
God only knows ; but this one thing we know, the
greater part of us, who are now in the house of God,

will be in an eternity of happiness or misery before the expiration of half a century. It concerns us all to reflect, for which of these states we are prepared—whether we are vessels of mercy preparing for glory, or vessels of wrath fitting for destruction.

What changes those of this audience will witness, who shall live fifty years from this time, is beyond human foresight. Whether the Federal union of these States will last half this time, is, from present appearances, very doubtful. But, according to the best received interpretation of ancient prophecies, the millennial state of the church will commence about that time.* We may rejoice in the anticipation of such a glorious event: but the eternal state of most of us will be fixed before the arrival of this period. It concerns us, one and all, to prepare ourselves for whatever may take place in the Divine government, while we shall be upon the stage of life. More especially it concerns us to prepare for our dissolution by death, from which no age is exempt. We who are old may be assured that our time on earth is short—that we must soon go the way whence none return—that the places which now know us on earth will know us no more. The greatest kindness we can extend to posterity, the greatest good we can do to those who may succeed us in our respective places, is, by a life of godliness and sobriety, to give our dying testimony for God and for religion. As we wish that posterity may enjoy the fruits of our labour, and reap the fields we have cultivated, let us teach them, by precept and example, to *fear*

* The Pope was formally invested with the authority of Universal Bishop by the Emperor Phocas, A. D. 606. Adding to this period, the 1260 days mentioned by Daniel, or, as is intended by prophetick days, 1260 years, we are brought to the year 1866.——*See Faber.*

4

God, to regard his *word*, his *day*, his *house*, his *wor-ship*, his *injunctions* of *justice*, *benevolence* and *charity*.

Finally—let it be the care of all to act their parts well on the stage of life, and to approve themselves faithful unto the death. May God of his mercy grant, that in the day of judgment we may meet together at the right hand of Jesus, and may be admitted into the kingdom of glory.——AMEN.

THE venerable Author of the above Sermon still lives. For his age, he possesses an unusual degree of bodily and mental strength; and, until the present time, (the fifty-eighth year of his ministry, and the eightieth of his life) he has been enabled, with little assistance, to perform all the duties of his office.

EDITOR.

Worcester, July, 1819.

CPSIA information can be obtained
at www.ICGtesting.com
Printed in the USA
BVHW04*1054170918
527708BV00015B/2220/P